Improving Care in the Community.

Tim Price

chipmunkapublishing
the mental health publisher

Tim Price

All rights reserved, no part of this publication may be reproduced by any means, electronic, mechanical photocopying, documentary, film or in any other format without prior written permission of the publisher.

>Published by
>Chipmunkapublishing
>United Kingdom

http://www.chipmunkapublishing.com

Copyright © Tim Price 2018

ISBN   978-1-78382-435-9

Also by Tim Price:
How to improve mental health
My insight   into the computing world
My Middlewich.
The changing world of mental health.
The Olympic Games 2012.
The Rio Olympic games 2016.

Improving Care in the Community.

How to Improve the World of Depression Services, Care Services and Resources, to Provide Care in the Community.

From a Depression and Asperger syndrome survivor.

Introduction
This book will try to suggest improvements to the services providing care. I will look, as a patient, how the service is now and how it used to be.
I used to be at South Cheshire College but I could not occupy myself when I was younger at South Cheshire college I can occupy myself now, I can do it very well indeed. I can now find my own education courses in the community education. This is a great change for me.
I would like to go on to higher education if possible. One day in the future but not yet because of writing books and enjoying it very much indeed. I would like to make it my career.

How I Became Depressed
I was fine at school, happy as can be but I became ill with depression when I left school at sixteen. I was coping very well but I tried to study engineering. I changed my mind when I was doing an engineering work placement at South Cheshire College. I first became depressed by not doing ordinary day to day things.

Services
I used the services to recover from the mental health issues and the staff dedicated their lives to help me to work towards getting better. I did not really plan to be ill in the first place with the mental health illness called depression.

Hospitals: How I recovered
Recovery was a slow process at first because I did not realise that I was ill but I ended up in hospital in Altrincham, on the outskirts of Manchester.

Tim Price

Altrincham Priory
I went into a private hospital called Altrincham Priory, I made a lot of friends   by visiting their rooms and helping them recover as well. As I was nearly better at 18 and a half years old. But I had a slight relapse in my depression when I left the hospital.
At Altrincham we took part in a variety of activities:
There was golf, swimming, art group, Zumba, yoga.
We went for walks to the video shop and the local library.
There was a number of nice walks in the grounds and one which went past Bryan Robson's house (he was my favourite Manchester United and England footballer, at the time.)
I left Altrincham Priory too early, in my opinion.
This was a fantastic hospital which nearly made me better.
I was better for six months but was admitted into Leighton Hospital when I was nineteen.

Leighton Hospital
I was admitted to Leighton hospital because I had a relapse in my depression. I was not myself at the time, I was getting worried about things I should not have been worrying about at all.
On day one I started to get better because I was put on the right sort of medication which helped.
I had an injection which settled me down and I started to get better. This was followed by tablets which I still take to help me.
We had a telly, good food, including fish and chips on Fridays. Great!
I came out of Leighton hospital when I was twenty years old.

Care in the Community
Gainsborough Road
When I came out of hospital I was placed in a group of three houses in Gainsborough Road, not far from the centre of Crewe. These were owned by the mental health team and used for rehabilitation purposes. They were ordinary semi-detached houses in a nice part of Crewe they were close to each other but not together.
They were used to provide a variety of experiences for mental health clients. They were essential to my recovery
The use of Gainsborough Road mental health buildings:

Improving Care in the Community.

121 was used for when a patient was discharged from hospital and the recovery process started and continued for me but not for some people they went back into hospital.
123 was used to continue the mental health recovery process of the world of care in the community. We went on holiday to different places around the country, such as Scotland and the Lake District.
54 was a flat more independent recovery. Clients had more responsibility, such as shopping and making some meals.

The Gainsborough road processes and procedures helped us on the road to recovery to eventually leave the buildings.
Unfortunately these facilities are no longer in use, they have been sold for private housing, and this was because of cuts to the budget which affected other parts of the service as well. A great shame because the Crewe service was the best. There was no better service around and there still isn't.
When Crewe and Nantwich Borough council became Cheshire East council the service was re-organised but not improved.

Fairburn Avenue

The mental health team bought a number of flats in Fairburn Avenue, near to Queens Park, for recovering clients to use.
The flats where very useful and they helped us to recover quicker than might otherwise have been the case.
The flats were needed to make us realise the way we all have different kinds of mental health issues and the world of improving education about the mental health issue called Depression and care in the community helped patients to improve.
Everybody in society can suffer from mental health issues.
I got ill because I was bored at home and I could not occupy myself properly, I needed to be in education and my friends did not realise I was going to be ill with depression I started to get ill after watching the Hillsborough semi-final between Liverpool and Nottingham Forrest in 1989. After watching the end of the semi-final at Sheffield on TV, I did not watch any football for a long time.

Life in the flats helped us recover quickly over time and with the help of dedicated health professionals, nurses and doctors helped us recover from our mental health issues.

Tim Price

The mental health team bought eight flats and a bungalow which was staffed twenty four hours a day at first. Each flat accommodated one person with mental health issues but they were assessed as being able to manage on their own, with help from staff.

The bungalow was for people who were unable to cope on their own because they needed more care from the professionals.

I was lucky I was allocated a flat which I have enjoyed. I really enjoy writing my books and doing my art work in my flat.

291 Centre (drop in centre)

There was also a resource centre in a large building on Nantwich Road, in Crewe. They had lots of facilities to help clients. They were great to get on with they had a pool table. I ran a pool team made up of clients. We played pool matches against other local centres, such as Chester.

We had great communication between staff and clients.

There was a kitchen, where I helped and a catering supervisor who helped me to get an NVQ in catering. She became the catering supervisor at Mill House in Nantwich in the bistro.

It worked very well because it was possible to learn from different people. There was a way to continue with different catering qualifications, if anyone needed to go further.

There was also a good deal of talking to each other and to staff. It was a proper working environment aimed at other clients.

I was very pleased when I got my NVQ certificate.

There were members' committee meetings every month. I was on the committee a few times.

There was far more work done on paper and pen, more work is done on the computer nowadays, all notes are processed on the computer using world processing. Notes were written by using a pen and paper. I did the notes for one meeting.

Patients' Notes

Everything is now computerised, I would prefer it if they were hand written. Today's National Health Service is not the same any more. There are great advantages of computerisation for agency care and general mental health care.

Improving Care in the Community.

Care Services in the Future
Improving education about mental health is essential. In general mental health education is about improving communication and knowledge about how to improve the diagnosis of mental health issues.
In the world of care in depression and care services the resources providing care in the community are important.
Providing essential care, knowledge and services for mental health is very important. Funding is vital.

Health Professionals
The world of educating the professionals about the mental health issue called manic depression or clinical Depression is very complex. Dedicated people help you to recover from Depression and the world of the depressive mind.
We must ensure that all doctors, consultants, nurses, etc. are trained to the highest standards in mental health. The government has the responsibility of ensuring that there are enough medical professionals to care for the population.
Care workers are also essential. They must be fully trained as well so that they can do their jobs effectively.
Care services, providing care in the community, are important to recovery.

Education
Schools, colleges and universities should teach their students and pupils about mental health. Teachers need more training and more awareness about mental health issues so that they can spot people who have conditions that might need help from professionals.

Police
The police need more awareness of mental health issues. Funding should be provided for training for this purpose.

Other Emergency Services
This applies to the whole range of emergency services, fire brigade, paramedics, first responders, etc.
Health professionals and others must have the awareness and training to deal with mental health issues.
This would help the care in the community policy of the government and the last government who have adopted this policy.

Tim Price

The care in the community in practice could be improved if there was a big effort to provide training and education for those involved.

Cuts in funding and therefore services have made it hard for the care in community policy to be effective. These cuts have been continuous under successive governments.

There needs to be another look at this.

The government's policies are not working properly because there have been too many cuts over several years resulting in a service which is not funded properly.

More research is required to provide a budget for the National Health Service, including proper provision for mental health education, care services and all resources.

The whole system needs to be reformed to provide a new care system.

New Care System

The care system should be based on research about what is the future of caring, what works and what does not. How can the service be improved for clients who have a mental health diagnosis.

How to expand the care services in an efficient but meaningful way for everyone involved.

There was a lot of good things happening twenty years ago, some of these should have been kept. They could be re-instated and the service consequently improved.

Where do patients who have just come out of hospital go?

There needs to be a place for respite and somewhere to be a recovery residential centre and a place for the clients to work.

There could be opportunities for work based training in a variety of jobs and services.

Rehabilitation Centres

I think that there should be places for people to live, with support, if required and opportunities for training, apprenticeships and recruitment in appropriate jobs.

This is very important. When patients are made better in hospital there needs to be a next stage to continue their process of getting well.

These could be big, or small, places where rehabilitation takes place. There needs to be sufficient research and funding to allow the building of appropriate places for care and rehabilitation.

Improving Care in the Community.

If the rehabilitation does not work it is important to have the necessary staff in place to deal with the situation.

Health and Care

Providing the help required in the world of services, providing care in depression and care services is vital. Resources must be provided to help people on the road to recovery. The different ways to improve the education about the mental health issues such as depression. Care services helping and providing the care needed to improve the services will be important.

Depression dependency sometimes means that people are reliant on medication, depending on personal circumstances.

Reliability, capability and understanding of the world of care services and resources is important in the changing world of depression and care in the community.

Recovery

This book will give an idea to people about how I used depression services and resources to recover from my depression. It took a long time to recover and get back to normal thinking.

Depression Services

I have seen this work first hand as a patient. The nurses, student nurses and doctors all work tirelessly together to help patients recover from their illnesses.

There are consultant doctors who specialise in a specific area of knowledge with high levels of qualifications.

This service needs to be extended and improved to provide provision for more care for more people. This will need more training for all levels, including apprenticeships and consultants. Newly trained staff and client volunteers will help.

The volunteers, depending on circumstances, if appropriate, could have the opportunity to train to be permanent staff. Volunteer first to see if the role is suitable, then undergo training to become professional carers. This would obviously not suit everyone but there would probably be a fairly large percentage of volunteers who would be interested in permanent jobs.

The levels of staffing would therefore be improved.

Tim Price

Care Services and Depression Services
It is essential to the recovery process for care and depression services to work together. There needs to be new centres built to replace existing, or closed buildings with appropriate new facilities which have staff who are properly qualified to help clients and patients. Care staff and depression awareness staff.

Improving
Hospital Admission and Care
If a patient can't get better they may have to be admitted to hospital, some may never come out of hospital. Most will recover and participate in rehabilitation in hospital and in the community.

Involvement
Involvement services would be involving patients in their recovery, in hospital admissions, patient care and care in the community. Patients will be involved at every stage, if they are well enough to participate in their care.

This happens now, to some extent but I think that there is a lot of scope for developing this approach to the benefit of present and future patients and staff.

Health and Social Care Reform
There must be a formula for funding health and social care education reforms. The Government, whoever is in charge, Conservatives or Labour, must ensure that the service is properly funded and staffed by people who are qualified in their chosen fields.

In addition clients who have got to know the system can help to improve the complete service.

Inspiring
Health and Social care services can be inspiring to people who have mental health issues and similar issues. The staff are dedicated people who care for patients and clients. They work with people to help them recover from their issues.

Education
The standard of education for staff, students, doctors, nurses and clients is vital.

Improving Care in the Community.

This must take place in schools, colleges, universities and training on the job, including apprenticeships. Actually doing the job will also contribute to the learning process.
This is very important.
Education should be provided for clients. This will take place in colleges, universities, hospitals, resource centres, recovery colleges and rehabilitation centres. The staff from the educational establishments could work in rehabilitation centres, as happened a few years ago for me in Crewe at the drop in centre.
The clients could gain qualifications if they wished, such as care and catering qualifications, NVQ, GNVQ. IT, English and Mathematics.
Leisure courses, such as Art, are also possible.

Rehabilitation
The services must be combined to provide appropriate care for clients. Care and health professionals must work together for the benefit of their colleagues and clients.

The Depressive Mind
When you think that you are going downhill towards a depressive mind and eventually to hospital admission, if needed. You should seek help as soon as possible from professionals.
It is important to occupy yourself at all times, especially when you are young.
The best way to occupy your mind is to carry on doing the things you always have, such as reading, listening to music, recording great music, walking and doing things with your friends.
Exercise is important and must be continued, if possible. The actual type of exercise is not important so long as you do it. Examples are walking, running, swimming and playing games, such as football. Swimming is particularly good because it uses all the muscles in your body.
Using your body and your mind is very good for your physical and mental health.

Tim Price

Photographs

I like taking photographs of my surroundings, including the sky, flowers, trees, lakes and everything around the countryside. Taking photographs is helpful in the process on the road to the recovery process of the depressive mind.

Recovery Process

How to improve the services and care in the community in the changing world of the depressive mind. The use of the recovery process, the provision of care services and resources is essential to enable clients and patients to improve their mental health so that they live a life to their full potential.

This needs full funding for services and resources to enable health professionals, doctors, nurses and consultants to improve the standards of care for the benefits of all patients and clients.

Activities should be provided in specialist places, as was the case twenty years ago in Crewe and Nantwich.

This would mean acquiring buildings to replace those that have been lost to the service.

Such as a day centre providing a variety of services:

Catering

Meetings

Day Trips

Holidays

Drop in centres

Christmas activities, Christmas dinner, parties, disco, etc.

Special themed days

Special catering events, such as meat and potato pie day and curry night.

Social events, such as

Cowboy and Indian day.

These were all provided by the local authority organisation, called Link.

Now Pass Care Limited, a private care service, client based, provide the care.

Pass Care Limited

Pass care limited replaced Link.

The care is paid for by direct payments.

I hope that one day my books will pay for my care.

I receive a visit for two hours on Tuesday when I cook, a variety of recipes, with staff curries and similar dishes are my favourite.

We also go for a brew and a cake in Costa coffee.

Improving Care in the Community.

I have another visit on Friday when staff do my ironing and some cleaning, if there is time.
Every fourth weekend I cook on the Saturday and go to Nantwich, Crewe, Nantwich canal centre or Minshull's garden centre for a brew on the Sunday.
The staff have also arranged some social activities such as a canal boat and pub lunch day trip, day to York National Railway Museum on a mini-bus and Christmas Dinner.
We do not go on holiday as we did with Link which is a shame. Pass Care is really a home based service.
Andrea, the joint manager at Pass Care Limited, comes to my CPA review meetings, together with my mum and dad.

Parents

My mum and dad help me a lot.
I spend three weekends out of four at home, in their house. We usually go out somewhere for lunch on Saturday and somewhere further afield on Sundays. Lately we have been to Middleport Pottery, Stoke on Trent, Middlewich, Little Moreton Hall, and Tatton Park.
One day a week, usually Wednesday, my dad (sometimes mum too when she is not working) comes over to my flat and spends about four hours with me, including a pub lunch and a coffee somewhere.
We go over to Nottingham several times a year to see my brother and his partner, Ann. When we are there we usually go to a park, or for a walk by the River Trent.
Every year we go to Wales for a weekend near the sea.
In March and October we go to Charlestown, Cornwall where we see my cousin, Tracie, her husband Fathi and her children, Charlotte, Heather and Adam. We visit lots of places, some of which we know well, such as Fowey, Mevagissey and Falmouth. As there are three of us we have agreed to choose two places each to visit during the week. I always choose Truro Cathedral and the Eden Project because I like them very much.
My mum and dad have their choices which vary, from a variety of National Trust properties, such as Lanhydrock to Penzance.
I like to take photographs of tourist attractions, flowers and lots of other things.

Tim Price

I used to go on canal holidays on our narrow boat, Slowcoach, with my mum and dad. I learned how to work the locks safely and actually became quite good at it.

We travelled to a lot of places along the canal system, including Nottingham, Worcester, Middlewich, Birmingham, Wigan, Northwich, Marple, Whaley Bridge and Burscough, which on the Leeds and Liverpool canal. I hope to go again, if staff approve.

Social Care Module

Social care has changed under this government and the previous one. A large section of the service has been privatised so that it is now unrecognisable from the one that existed in the 1980s.

The service was better before privatisation, mainly because of funding.

I would like to see it back to as is it was before, or even better. This will mean the Government making more funds available to local authorities and the National Health Service.

Improvements are necessary in the provision of health care professionals, such as nurses, doctors and consultants. There needs to be a new building programme.

Research into care is vitally important to improve the system. There has not been sufficient funding over many years by several governments. Some GP services have been privatised as have many other services.

We are still spending money when necessary on some parts of the service.

Patients, clients and staff all deserve a better deal.

This would mean more funding to provide better pay and conditions, including pensions, for all NHS staff. Less privatisation to provide a better service. Not complete privatisation as this Government appears to want.

The buildings should improve and new ones purchased and built. With regard to mental health we need better facilities and resources to provide care for all patients and clients.

There needs to be a lot more staff to cater for the clients and buildings.

Hospital wards should be provided, near to all towns and cities, for all mental health requirements. This is important, friends and family should not have to travel too far to see their loved ones.

Public transport is not a very good way to travel to a hospital visit nowadays because of the cutbacks to services.

Improving Care in the Community.

There needs to be more funding for public transport, buses, trains and trams in cities and towns. This would also help the environment because there would be less pollution from petrol and diesel cars.
Electric buses and trams would also reduce pollution. There are a lot of electric trains but not on all tracks yet.
Above all there needs to be a good service for everyone, twenty four hours a day, including holiday time.
This would be in addition to better local mental health and care facilities.
There needs to be a continuation of some of the old working practices and the introduction of new ones, where appropriate.
This also applies to services and resources, such as buildings for clients.

Education and Care
The way we continue to educate the clients, patients and staff is vital to the future of care services, providing the care needed in the United Kingdom and around the world.
The changing ways education for care is provided in the care services, health and social care and mental health care provision is very important.
In the future of the world of care services provision, providing adequate care services and care must be done.
Educating the professionals must be an important addition to the process.
Educational resources are vital in the recovery process in the world of depressive mind. How to recover from the issues of the depressive persons mind.
The education about the world of the depression mind and the recovery process and the procedure of the recovery world of the depressive mind.
All people involved must thoroughly understand the issues.

Recovery Processes of the depressive mind
The future of the depressive mind and the way we deal with clinical Depression and the recovery process and the procedure of how we live and deal with the mental health issue called Depression.

Tim Price

The way we deal with the recovery process in the world of the person with the depressive mind and how we use the health care service is very important to everybody concerned in this context.
Recovery is possible if you are determined to succeed to make it work. If you do not try at all you will not succeed.
You have to do it yourself but it helps if you have the support of family friends and staff.

Hospital Admission

The first thing to say is that hospitals are essential to the recovery process. Without them patients have got no chance of recovery. There is a need for mental health beds in all areas.
There is also a need for paramedic services, staffed by people who are qualified to cope with the issues.
I needed to be in hospital twice before I was properly better. Once in Altrincham Priory and then in Leighton Hospital for a year.
There are currently insufficient beds for mental health patients, this is because of consistent cutting of funding, over the years, by successive governments.
The future of mental health care is not looking great.

Using the Services Available

The world of the depressive person or patient and the use of the services and resources available at the time they are needed is very important.
Whatever the issues, whether hospital admission is required or not, patients, staff and clients must use the resources and services available at the time.

Music and Other Soothing Sounds

How we use music to recover from the depressive mind. Listening and playing music can help depressed people to recover. The sound of birds singing and the sea's waves lapping on the shore will also help to make people better.
I have had experience of these sounds which did make me better but I did not realise at the time because I was too young at seventeen.
I did enjoy the experience.
I was told to listen to music by a fellow pupil, she was correct.
I still listen to music a lot and I love listening to the waves when I am in Cornwall, or anywhere by the sea.
The sound of the sea hitting the sand on the beach is very relaxing.

Improving Care in the Community.

I enjoy this very much indeed.
I love 1960s music, such as the Beatles, Rolling Stones, Cliff Richard and the Shadows. I also like Kylie Minogue (I have been to see her three times at the Manchester Evening News Arena). Erasure are also another of my favourites.
I listen to lots of other singers and recording artists, such as the Pet Shop Boys and Depeche Mode.
Simply Red are also one of my favourites, I have all their CDs.
In the evening I quite often play music to relax.

Patient Care
There must be funding available for proper patient care.
There must be thorough research into mental health provision and care in the community, there must be a proper funded service which is well managed.
This is important and must include General Practitioners, other health professional, consultants and mental health wards, which must be near to all towns, supported accommodation, fully staffed and other accommodation with supervision from qualified people.
We used to have mental health wards in Leighton Hospital for Crewe and surrounding areas. These wards were closed with local patients having to move to Macclesfield for in patient mental health treatment.
Community care services and resources have been privatised with a lack of coordination of the services involved.
This mental health provision is inadequate for the area.
Mental health patients need and deserve a better service which is coordinated from GP services, when first ill to full recovery medication, care and all other resources must be coordinated with appropriate funding.
Research is important in the field so the best treatment is available, at all times to all patients.
Mental health is a Worldwide issue, funding should be found everywhere.
It would be good to find the best practices in other countries.

Holidays, Trips and Visits
Since Link closed down in Crewe the clients only have home visits by staff. There is no longer the opportunity to go on holiday, as a group. Not even day trips and visits.
We are very much on our own, apart from the home visits.

Tim Price

The Ideal
I would like to see the following:
Visits to different local places like the National Trust houses.
Museums.
Art Galleries.
Zoos
Important historical places, such as Chester.

Holidays
There should be the opportunity for group holidays to places like The Lake District, the Seaside, North Wales, Somerset and other holiday destinations.

Depression and Care Services
Depression and care services are essential to the recovery process. The world of any person who suffers from depression eventually becomes different than the world of other people.
There is a need for better funding, from the beginning of the illness, getting depressed and eventually to the recovery process of the depressive mind.

Recovery Process in Detail
The first step when you are not very well is to make an appointment with your General Practitioner who will make a referral to a mental health consultant.
Admission to a hospital may happen, if the consultant thinks it is necessary and appropriate.
This will mean going into hospital.
Consultants, doctors, nurses and others will try (and succeed in most cases) to make you better.
When you are ready there needs to be accommodation, in all districts, with support of specialised staff to suit rehabilitation.
This could be ordinary houses, or specialised accommodation with support when required. Patients have the ability to look after themselves, if possible, but there needs to be support, if needed.
The patients need to go on to their own flat, or house. Staff should be available if required. Twenty four hours a day, all year round. Ideally nearby.
Staff support must be provided.
All people involved should be properly trained, staff and clients.

Improving Care in the Community.

Depression and Mental Health Care

The depressive mind and how the world of the person with the mental health issue called depression can be dealt with by the patient is important.

How the recovery process and procedure of the care services and resources in the future combine is also important. The patients must take part in the recovery process, if they want to be involved, not everybody does.

Depressive care services and mental health care by professionals can help patients to recover, if they want to recover. Clinical depression can be usually treated quicker that manic depression. Medication can help those patients who are clinically and manically depressed.

The World of the Depressive Mind

A person who is clinically depressed is usually very ill. They are medically depressed and often reliant on medication.

Ordinary people need to realise that we are talking about an illness which, over time, will get better but, often lives will change. This is very important.

This is very true for most people but not for all, sadly, some have committed suicide.

The majority go on to lead normal lives, treatment works for most people. They need to continue to have care, however. Their lives are never quite the same.

Some patients and ex patients can set up their own successful businesses. Some are unable to do anything because of heavy medication.

Exercise and Mental Health

Exercise is essential to the recovery process. If you don't exercise you could have an early death.

Any kind of exercise is important, you must keep active. This can be hard when you leave school because of the change of routine. Swimming, walking, running, gym work, football and other games, are all ok for exercise during the recovery process. As long as you do some exercise every day and keep it up.

Tim Price

Diet

Eating good food, fruit (apples, bananas, strawberries, grapes, and oranges), vegetables, chicken, fish, wholemeal bread and similar things are good for your physical and mental health.

Alcohol should be limited to small quantities, a couple of pints or glasses of wine. Whiskey and other spirits should be kept for special occasions.

It is possible to cook your own meals with fresh ingredients, with help from staff, if necessary.

Shopping for fresh ingredients is important, this can be done at any shop or supermarket. Beef, lamb and chicken are readily available which can be combined with a variety of sauces to make nice meals. Vegetables can be added to make better meals.

One of my favourite meals is minced beef curry which I like to cook, with the help of staff, and eat with rice, or on its own.

For breakfast I have toast which I make from wholemeal bread.

I have five pieces of fruit a day.

Depressive Person and Mental Health Care

You do not need to be ill at first to become depressed.

You do not necessarily realise that you are ill. It is not obvious but can become so over time.

One of the most important things is to realise that there is a problem. It is not often obvious to doctors and consultants.

If they do not realise that there is a problem you can be sent home because they do not realise that there is an issue.

It is possible, if you do not keep yourself well, for illness to return. Diagnosis and treatment is vital.

Treatment and Recovery Process

Treatment can help the recovery process. Reaction to medication can prolong the mental health process, however.

The quicker treatment is accessed the better.

Medication, Mental Health Care and Exercise

Medication is an important part of mental health care but it is not everything for the recovery process.

Physical fitness is important because the fitter you are the better your mental health will be, in the long term.

So try to get as much exercise as possible. It does not matter what exercise you do, so long as you do some.

Examples are: swimming, athletics, walking, running, gym work, cycling, playing sport, including walking football, etc.

Improving Care in the Community.

Relaxation is important too, there are specialist music tracks to help. There are also tracks featuring sounds of the sea and birdsong.

Massage
Massage with special oils can help you to relax. It helps your skin to recover from day to day stresses.
It is essential to mental health care and helps the recovery/rehabilitation process.
It is a good opportunity for students who are studying massage to work with mental health people and help their wellbeing.

The Whole Depression Services
The depressive person sometimes can develop the illness quite late in life. You can develop the problem without knowing and without realising. Over time your life style can develop the problem with lots of health issues.

Mental Health and Care Services
Mental health care services have changed, not for the better, for the worse. Privatisation has been widely introduced by successive governments which has resulted in the downgrading of services in the National Health Service.
Education services have been cut back for the same reason.
Cuts in funding have resulted in the downgrading of all mental health services across the country. This has affected resources such as buildings, staff and clients in an adverse way.
Some people are finding it very hard.
The way the services have changed all around the country is because of the funding. Research is funded in different ways resulting in poorer care in care in the community.

The Whole System of Depression Care
The depressive mind is the main focus of this book, together with the recovery process procedure.
The system needs to be reformed and funded properly with adequate education which is so important to complete the recovery process.
Recovery services in the community are different than hospital mental health services which are very complex.

Tim Price

The Government is relying on less hospital admissions which means more community care and therefore more workers with client based knowledge. The improvements and changes to the system has meant that the organisation has been re vamped and is now profit making.

Business and mental health

Profit making is an essential part of privatisation and is therefore about money which impacts on the care services. There are less services for clients and patients.

The privatisation process is an example of the way society has become money orientated and services have become market driven.

This means clients and patients receive less services for less money.

The service is ok, for the money which is less. The idea is more services for less money.

People who suffer from depression are in the middle of this situation and treatment can help patients to recover.

Some people do not get better, they do not even try. Some commit suicide and some stay in hospital for ever. Privatisation does not help.

Funding for Mental Health

It is essential that the funding that is allocated to mental health treatment and research, is actually spent on mental health and not on other National Health Services. This "ring fencing" of mental health funds is important.

Services to Help the Recovery Process

The services that used to exist are no longer available, they are no longer there. There used to be a number of services to help patients and clients who have clinical depression and other mental health issues.

These included 291, a large Victorian house where we could meet and socialise and help with catering. South Cheshire College came to 291 to teach clients in various ways.

The College taught clients:

Information and Communication Technology,

English,

Mathematics,

Catering NVQ

Improving Care in the Community.

Health and Safety
Health and Hygiene
And other courses.
The idea of having the FE College to help was excellent and benefitted all clients who took part and their staff.

The Future of Education

I would like to study ICT level 2 but the college do not have the funding.
Clients now have to arrange and fund their own education.
Funding should be provided for adult education.
There is a need to improve the education system for people with mental health issues.
Accessing the services available for the depressive mind can be an issue for clients and patients. Staff can also develop these issues.

The Services Available
The depressive mind and care services

The depressive mind can develop from not doing things over a period of time. If the situation deteriorates help may be required, including hospital admission.
Accessing great services is a vital part of recovering from the depressive mind.
The provision of care services is important for clients and patients and must be effective.
The care services that were in place in Crewe were the best in the country. They are still good but because of cuts there is less and less available to patients.
There are now brand new services for depression.
The services need more funding and research to improve education and thus make the system more effective.

The Care Profession (Education)

Education is very important for all care professionals. There is a need for a new health and social care commission to ensure that the right funding is available for education and research for all care staff.
Training which could be at university, apprenticeships or training on the job, is vital to improve standards of care in the profession.
Clinical Depression can be treated with self-help but it needs educated professionals to work with clients and patients.

Tim Price

The world of education and the way we deal and live with the mental health issue called Depression is important.

The care profession and depression services are provided to help the person, client or patient recover from the mental health issue called depression.

Clinical depression service and care provision provided over the years and the changing world of depression and care services provided in hospitals all around the country.

Social care and depression awareness courses provided in the first place in hospital admission if it is required. The world of the depressive person and the way the person reacts to medication if it is needed to help the person recover from the mental health issue called clinical depression.

The depressive aspect of the recovery process and the services and resources available in the world of the depressive person, patient, client or member of the national health service in the care profession is very important.

The standards of care in the community in the future of the world of depression services and resources and care services. In the changing world of depression and care in the community the future of improving the lives of patients and clients in the world of depression services is vital.

The community of care.

The future of the changing world of depression and the world of care services in the world of care in the community.

A lot of people who are clients and patients are friendly to each other in the community. When I was in hospital at Altrincham Priory I was friendly with lots of other patients and used to go round to see them as much as possible.

When I was in Link it was a drop in service which meant that I used to see a lot of people, clients, patients and staff on a regular basis.

There was training on the job and regular clients' meetings.

The changing world of depression and the services and care in the changing way the depression services or used to improve the knowledge of the developing functioning depressive mind of the changing world of the depressive person and the road to recovery using services and resources providing care and care in the community. And the world of the depressive mind and depression and care services and daily care provided in the changing world of the depressive mind.

Improving Care in the Community.

Depression services
Depression services are being improved through Care in the Community. This service has been changed because there are more services and less money.

Services should be funded properly and be adequate for the staff, clients and patients' needs.

People live their lives according to what they think they can achieve according to their ability and capability.

Finance and mental health are linked but need more research at all levels.

The future of care services and depression services
This needs an improvement in education and care services available to the client and patient.

It would benefit from the expansion of education for all people involved, including staff, patients and clients. This would be delivered by all sectors, universities, colleges, schools and even nurseries.

This is very important and must be done if there is to be a successful service.

The Service in the Future
In the future I think that there will be more services that are paid for by the individual client, or patient.

There will be less staff to do the work.

This is happening now.

Education
The education system for mental health care and services in future must improve and be appropriate for the new system. This will impact on the standards of care that are available for parents, clients and patients.

Rehabilitation Services
The whole care system needs to be reformed with education being an important part of this.

Rehabilitation services are now inferior to those of twenty years ago.

In Crewe the drop in service at 291 has been sold as a private house. This was part of an excellent service in Crewe run by the

Borough Council prior to Local Government reorganisation. There was adequate services and staff who worked well with clients to improve mental health knowledge and skills.

There was also Macon House, which has recently burnt down, which was used as administration offices and care services for people with special needs.

There were three rehabilitation houses in Gainsborough Road, Crewe, which were used when patients were discharged from hospital.

They worked well for me but not for some people who had to return to hospital.

These three houses have now been sold and not replaced.

They were judged to be surplus to requirements and therefore not retained.

This was a political decision which was a mistake, in my opinion. There was a local campaign to keep these facilities but it was not successful.

Depression and Resources for Care

Depression services and resources are essential for care in the world of depression.

The expansion of care services and education would increase the knowledge of everybody in the care system.

The care system is changing. There is less money to provide the same services.

More people are using the services but there is less money available to provide these services.

It is a lot worse now than twenty years ago. More money was available to provide care.

Many services have been privatised.

The changing care system has resulted in less service because of cuts to mental health funding.

The future of the world of depression and care services and resources is dependent on funding, research and education.

This needs finance from the local authority and the National Health Service. Above all the Government.

The allocation of sufficient finance is very important.

The national government of the day are ultimately responsible. I would like to see an expansion of care which will need more money.

Improving Care in the Community.

Fitness and Sport
Depression can be helped by exercise and sport. Taking part in sport can help patients to enjoy their leisure in full and recover quickly.
Physical exercise, such as walking, swimming, running, playing games, such as football, are important for the well-being of everyone, including patients.
Athletics is a good way to keep fit and good for the mind too. Watching sport is good too because it helps clients to relax.
Depression can be helped by playing sport in sporting teams and teaching football. This helps in the recovery process and the world of depression and care.
Patients play the game of football and enjoy playing football to the best of their footballing capability and football understanding. There is now walking football for older people.
The game itself can change mental health care. Professional and amateur players can suffer from mental health issues.
Playing sport definitely helps in the world of depression. Care services can improve the standards in the world of playing great football all around the world.
All sport can have people who have mental health issues. There have been many sports people who have developed mental health problems.
There must be awareness of mental health issues in the community which can be helped by better education at all levels.
This applies to sport and mental health in general.
People need to recover as soon as possible with the help of health professionals in the mental health community.
How to deal and live with depression symptoms is vital to the recovery process.

Care and Continuous Depression Services
There is a need for care services to continue throughout clients' and patients' mental health issues. This needs staff input occasionally. Patient based services, re organisation and care in the community.
Improving the world of depression, care services and resources in the care system for depression clients, patients and staff.
Training on the job, including apprenticeships, and other courses at colleges, schools and universities is very important.

The process is an important part of education and improved care in the community system.

The resources for care in the community need to expand for the improvement of all patients, clients and staff.

The world of depression has changed.

There is now much more care in the community than there was and less mental health hospital beds (although I think that hospital admission is an important part of the rehabilitation process).

The service is provided by private care companies because of the local authority cut backs, Councils and the NHS are unable to provide a full service now.

These private companies are often organised by people who used to work for Local Authorities, so they can improve care services and the life of clients, patients and staff.

The private companies, together with some public provision, will continue to provide adequate health care, using health professionals of all types.

Future Role of Depression and Care Services

The future will be better with an injection of cash to provide a fully funded service for all clients and patients.

This should include the re-opening of psychiatric wards, or building new ones so that no patient has to travel for more than fifteen minutes from their home to a hospital bed.

Care in the community for mental health should include support for all patients, including a CPN and a consultant.

The future of mental health will inspire people to work in mental health care. These people will come from other areas and be trained, on the job, or from university.

There should be apprenticeships as part of on the job training to gain knowledge and skill. These people should be working to improve services in all respects.

New staff are needed from a variety of training sources.

When they are trained they are inspiring to work with.

Home Care Team

The Home Care Team is a link between the hospital and the community. They help with the recovery process, including the use of medication and dedicated carers, nurses and doctors. All health care professionals.

Improving Care in the Community.

They travel around to different parts of the area to chat to clients and to supervise their medication. This is to help people to recover and to make sure that their medication is taken at the right time and that the right amount is used.
This helps the process of recovery and modular care.

Depression and Care Services
There are various care services available to patients, clients and staff. This involves training on the job, knowledge of care services and work experience in hospital and in the community.
This also means improving education knowledge and mental health awareness. Client awareness is important to improve the standards of care across the mental health sector and help from health professionals.
Client knowledge is an important element of care. Clients must understand their situation and why they need care in the community.
Health and safety knowledge is very important to mental health care, including in the community. This will help to prevent accidents for clients and staff in their daily roles and careers in health and social care work.
All clients benefit from the care they receive from health professionals and care assistants, both in hospital and in the community.

Continuation of Health and Social Care
The care service must continue at all stages of mental health issues. Social care is vital to look after clients and patients. Social care needs to be properly funded following thorough research and there needs to be adequate facilities across the country, even the World.
In Crewe there used to be very good modular social care and facilities.
The service has now been privatised by successive governments. These companies are primarily interested in profit, the opposite of 1948 when the National Health Service was formed.
The NHS was started by the Attlee Labour Government and it was a free service for everybody. It has changed over the years but was still free in principle until recently when successive governments changed things.

The governments needed more money so they increased charges for various services, including dental and eye care.

Services for mental health are now privately run, to some extent from public funds.

Health and Social Care

In January 2018 the Prime Minister, Theresa May, re-appointed Jeremy Hunt as Health Secretary but added Social Care to his title. He should also have the title of Mental Health Secretary in my opinion.

The job of Mental Health Secretary should have been started in the 1980s when Mrs Thatcher, the Iron Lady, was in charge.

Jeremy Hunt is responsible for mental health but he does not have it as a title. He should.

He really should be replaced by someone who can combine the roles of Health, Social Care and Mental Health. This would improve the services and the future of care would be much better.

Research is necessary to determine the amount of new funding required for health, social care and mental health

There is no doubt in my mind that there is a need for a lot more funding for mental health services.

There should also be more teaching of mental health in schools, colleges and universities. Apprenticeships would also be a useful addition which would enable training on the job.

The Care System in the Future

The care system has been the same for twenty years (I covered this in my previous two books about mental health, "How to Improve Mental Health" and "The Changing World of Mental Health", available from chipmunkapublishing.co.uk)

The care system is changing so that the format of mental health care is funded differently. The whole National Health Service needs more research and funding.

The Brexit procedure may affect the system. It may be better, it may be worse.

Hopefully it will be better because the system needs more care and funding and Brexit could deliver enough cash to improve the NHS. But there might be less money.

There will have to be new ideas in a Finance Bill to fund the future of care in the community.

The care system needs improving and education needs to get better. Politicians, of all parties, are important to ensure that

Improving Care in the Community.

education and improvement in the system actually happens. They are beginning to improve the political system with regard to mental health. This is a good thing.
Education about mental health is important to improve children's lives. There needs to be proper funding, research and knowledge. Mental health education is improving people's knowledge and knowhow about the problems and patient care services.
Members of Parliament can improve mental health awareness. Mental health care needs to be reviewed to improve education for all.
A lot of MPs have now take a particular interest in mental health care, including our local MP, for Crewe and Nantwich, Laura Smith.
Care services need improvement for mental health clients and patients. MPs and health professionals will try to improve education and resources.
Privatisation of the National Health Service will not help.

Education and Children's Services
Mental Health care is important. To improve education of all pupils and students there needs to be a change to mental health education and care.
This should be part of schools', colleges' and universities' curriculum and employment training, jobs and apprenticeships. The education system needs improving so that pupils, students and therefore everybody is more aware of the issues surrounding mental health and are happy to talk about them just as they would talk about issues of physical health.
School pupils are quite likely to experience mental health problems because of the stresses of school.
Teachers in schools, colleges and universities need to improve their support from health professionals, social care services and community care staff.
This is important to improve services to teachers, pupils and students.
Mental health care services must be provided in educational establishments so that there is a noticeable improvement in care for all in schools, colleges and universities. There should be access to health care professionals who will provide proper care.
They will improve education and knowledge for everybody involved in the education process.

Tim Price

Mental health care is important in every school, college and university.
It needs improving and would be with changes to the system, such as I have suggested.
There needs to be a link between all schools, colleges and universities because it is essential that mental health knowledge about individual students is shared between all educational institutions.
This will help to improve mental health for all students and pupils, clients and patients.

Resources in the Future

Funding must be greater in the future. Better use should be made of technology such as social media, computers and information technology.
Training will also be important including apprenticeships leading to jobs.
Schools, colleges and universities will all have a part to play.
Mental health care is very important.
There must be more research to find resources to replace the old care system.
Buildings must be replaced and rebuilt if necessary to provide suitable accommodation for clients and facilities where they can discuss their needs with appropriate staff.
Mental health hospital beds are important to the recovery process, therefore there must be funding to provide adequate beds for mental health patients. This will mean building new accommodation in some cases, or changing the use of existing beds to mental health provision.
Every sizeable hospital should have mental health wards properly staffed.
Patients, clients, their family and friends should not have to travel too far to visit people in hospital. It should be possible to use buses and trains and other forms of public transport to get to the hospital in a short time.
The future of care needs to be reviewed and properly funded. This will improve the communication between patients, clients and health care professionals, social workers, nurses and doctors.
Everyone, clients and staff, deserve the best.
Facilities to improve mental health care, places to talk/socialise and should include a relaxation room, kitchen, gym, swimming pool, outside recreation area, gardens.

Improving Care in the Community.

These could be used for exercise, catering, gardening, swimming, walks.

My Ideal Mental Health Rehabilitation Centre
In my opinion the ideal centre for rehabilitation would include:
Bedrooms with own bathroom.
It is important that clients have their own area. These rooms should be looked after and cleaned properly.
Day and night care facilities.
Twenty four hour care is important for some people but others can manage. It is not essential.
Kitchen
There must be a kitchen to enable clients to cook their meals, if they are capable. This should be healthy fresh food.
Gym
A gym would provide the opportunity for exercise which would, together with the good food, help clients to have a healthy lifestyle.
Swimming pool.
Swimming is really good exercise which would help fitness.
Catering services.
Meals could be provided by outside caterers or in house.
Relaxation room.
It helps to be able to relax. Lighting is important here.
Garden
Walking around gardens, enjoying plants, growing flowers is very relaxing.
Quiet room
A quiet room is for very quiet activities such as reading.
Eating room.
This is a new way of replacing the dining room with a multipurpose facility where clients are able to eat their meals and snacks.
Talking room
This would a room for teaching and learning about mental health. Recovery would be improved by this procedure. Talking to each other about mental health would also be possible.
Staff would lead this talking.
Activities section.

Tim Price

This would be sporting events, such as walking, football, swimming, and gardening, etc. There would opportunities for day trips (see below).

Day Trips

This could include, Blackpool, Liverpool Beatles Museum, Television Museum, and Football Museums, Chester city and cathedral, National Trust places, Special places in the National Trust. Day trips are important for recovery.

It would also be good to go on a canal day trip, calling at the pub, or a picnic on the boat.

Visits around the local area would also be good (there are a lot of places of interest in Stoke on Trent, such as pottery factories and museums.

Mental health services

There must be access to all professional medical staff, nurses, doctors, consultants, trained health care assistants for all clients and patients.

They must all have their own rooms to see patients and clients. Ward should also be available.

Mental health courses.

There would be social care courses to improve education for all patients and clients. This would improve mental health awareness and help clients to recover.

Mental health reception

It is good to have a responsive reception team who are friendly, efficient and easy to talk to.

Mental health CPA meetings.

These are important to improve services and care for clients and staff. There must be appropriate rooms available for these vital meetings.

Holidays

This would give plenty of opportunity for exercise which is very important for mental health recovery.

These would be in different places, hotels, self-catering cottages, boats, etc. It would be good to get to know people.

Holidays could be in lots of places such as Blackpool, Cornwall, Somerset, Morecombe, Scotland, Wales, Lake District, France and other places.

There would also be appropriate care services and resources for all clients and patients. People would be able to come in for the day.

Improving Care in the Community.

Building
The care service would need new buildings to replace those that have been demolished, or used for other purposes, such as private housing.
These new buildings would have all the facilities necessary, as described above.

Articles about mental health.
Writing new books about mental health care services and resources and care in the community is important.
Articles in newspapers and magazines are important to write to inform and educate the general public and clients about mental health issues and developments.
Writing on the internet, on Facebook, Twitter and other platforms is an important to improve mental health services.

Recovering from Depression
The changing world of depression and care services and the way the world of depression services help people recover from the mental health issues called manic depression and the world of clinical depression. The care profession, care work and social care work is changing. It is important that these systems improve.

The Care Profession and Mental Health Care
The health care professionals are important to the recovery process. The ones I have come into contact with have been great, they have helped me a lot over the years and are still doing so. Health assistants, nurses, doctors and consultants have all been good in the process of helping me to recover.
The Community Health teams are important resources and are likely to become more important in the future so that patients can be cared for in their own homes and not in hospital.
They are vital to the success of mental health treatment in the future.
The future of the service may well be different with stronger local teams and less hospital admissions.
Improving education about the mental health issues called manic depression and clinical depression is very important .The care of depression in the community in the future will hopefully change for the better. Funding must be adequate.

Tim Price

Young People and Children
The first signs of mental health issues are often when people are young so there is a need for more care and funding for younger people.

Funding
Funding of mental health services is essential to the process of recovery.

Care in the Community, Replacement Care Module
There is a need for a replacement module of community care. This is the way the service will operate in the future.

My Books
I am now an author, writing books about different subjects like mental health in general, care services, the world of depression and care in the community.

I write books to inspire people to improve education about the world and about care services providing care in Depression and care modules of the future way of educating the world about Depression and care in the changing world of care. Services and resources.

Conclusion
Any person can become depressed at any time in their life. There are different ways to recover from the mental health issues called manic depression and clinical depression.

The way the recovery process is acted on the depressive mind and the road to the complete recovery from depression, so that they don't need the services anymore and help others to recover more quickly.

In the future the awareness of mental health care services and resources providing care needed to start the client's recovery will be important.

Recovery from mental health issues is usually possible if clients, staff and patients work together to enable complete recovery from depression.

Care in the community helps people to recover from a diagnosis of clinical depression. This means contact with social workers,

Improving Care in the Community.

consultants and carers. Resources are essential to the process. At the time of writing this book, more resources are needed.
Care services in the community with a module of care will help the person to recover from the mental health issue in the first place.
The future of learning and teaching about mental health knowledge and the future of continuing the world of care services is about providing care when needed. Providing the possibility of hospital admission if it is required or even needed.
Research is important to improve services and care. This will only be possible if there is sufficient funding for staff to do the work. Hopefully the government will make the necessary finance available.
Care services in health and social care need working on to ensure a proper service is provided. This will need proper funding by the NHS from the government. Community care services will therefore be improved for the whole community.
 Changes in mental health care are inspiring the way to improve the education of mental health courses and social care in the community.
The government must provide the funding for their mental health commitment to back it up. People can have any mental health problems at any time.
The vast majority of people can recover from mental health problems, with the correct support and from community teams.
When I came out of hospital, in 1993, there was houses, flats, wards and a drop in centre. It was an excellent standard of care in hospital, the community and mental health team work.
I would like to see the same standards patients and clients today.

www.ingramcontent.com/pod-product-compliance
Ingram Content Group UK Ltd.
Pitfield, Milton Keynes, MK11 3LW, UK
UKHW041413180426
11947UKWH00007B/114